RAILWAYS OF THE CHILTERNS

Patrick Bennett

AMBERLEY

First published 2021

Amberley Publishing
The Hill, Stroud
Gloucestershire, GL5 4EP

www.amberley-books.com

Copyright © Patrick Bennett, 2021

The right of Patrick Bennett to be identified as
the Author of this work has been asserted in
accordance with the Copyrights, Designs and
Patents Act 1988.

ISBN 978 1 4456 9918 9 (print)
ISBN 978 1 4456 9919 6 (ebook)

British Library Cataloguing in Publication Data.
A catalogue record for this book is available from
the British Library.

Typesetting by Aura Technology and Software
Services, India. Printed in the UK.

Contents

Introduction

To the north and north-west of London lies a band of hills, the Chilterns. These chalk hills, 45 miles long and up to 12 miles deep, stretch from Goring-on-Thames, Oxfordshire, to Hitchin, Hertfordshire. In a number of places, the hills reach to more than 850 feet above sea level. It was an unfortunate fact for the early railway companies that those building a line heading out of London in a northerly or north-westerly direction had to surmount these hills.

First on the scene in 1838 was the London & Birmingham Railway, later to form part of the London & North Western Railway. The digging of the 2½-mile long cutting through the chalk at Tring ruined the contractor undertaking the work. Next on the scene was the Great Northern, which competed its line in 1850. The Great Western opened a line to High Wycombe in 1854, which was extended to Oxford in 1864. The Midland finally reached London on its own tracks in 1868.

The Metropolitan started out as an underground railway in London. It gradually extended out into the countryside, establishing 'Metroland' in the process. Harrow on the Hill was reached in 1880, Amersham in 1889, and Aylesbury in 1892. The Great Central was a late arrival on the scene. It first reached its terminus at Marylebone in 1899, partly using Metropolitan Railway tracks. Later a second route was added via the Great Western's High Wycombe line. This opened in 1906.

As well as these five main lines there were numerous branch lines, acting both as feeders to the main lines and also providing the means of making cross-country journeys without the need to access the capital. Sadly, all but two of these branch lines have closed, although a short section of one has reopened as a preserved line. To the north of the Chilterns, making a link between all five of the main lines, was the Oxford–Cambridge line. Only the sections between Bletchley and Bedford and between Bicester and Oxford remain open, but there are plans to reinstate the whole line, although this is a very long-term project.

The five main lines are treated in turn, working from the London end northwards. Each is then followed by the images and descriptions of the branch lines which radiate from them. The Hertford, Luton & Dunstable Railway, and the Oxford to Cambridge line are followed from east to west.

Acknowledgements

The author and publisher would like to thank the following people for permission to use copyright material in this book: Peter Lovell for the photographs taken at Northchurch (2), Soulbury, Oddington (2), High Wycombe (3), Saunderton (2), and Princes Risborough (2); Peter Groom for the photographs taken at Wood Green (2), Hadley Wood, Hatfield, Radlett, Bedford, Marylebone, and Moor Park; the Railway Correspondence and Travel Society (RCTS) for the photographs taken at Bletchley (2), Bedford (3), Winslow, Verney Junction, Claydon, Houghton Regis, Croxley Green, Potters Bar, Hitchin (2), Sandy, Harpenden East, Elstree, Leagrave, Redbourn, Princes Risborough, Rickmansworth, Aylesbury and Quainton Road; the Science Museum for the pictures taken at Kings Langley, Tring, Bletchley (2), Denbigh Hall and St Pancras; the London North Western Railway Society for the photographs taken at Watford Junction, Boxmoor, Tring, Bletchley (2), Leighton Buzzard, Stanbridgeford and St Albans.

The photographs by Ben Brooksbank taken at Hatch End, Berkhamsted, Northchurch, Tring (2), Cheddington (2), Bletchley, Welwyn, Hitchin (3), Elstree, Radlett, Leagrave, Harlington, Millbrook, Bedford, Sharnbrook, Heath Park, Seer Green, Neasden, Chalfont and Latimer and Amersham; the photographs taken by Lamberhurst at Bletchley, Bedford, Verney Junction, Leighton Buzzard, Hertingfordbury, Nast Hyde, Wotton, Thame (2), Wheatley, Horspath, Aston Rowant, Bledlow Bridge, and Kingston Crossing; the photograph taken at Bedford by Geoffrey Skelsey; the photograph taken by Barry Lewis at Luton, and the photograph taken by Matt Buck at St Albans are reproduced under the Creative Commons Share Alike License. Every attempt has been made to seek permission for copyright material used in this book. However, if we have inadvertently used copyright material without permission/acknowledgement we apologise and will make the necessary correction at the first opportunity.

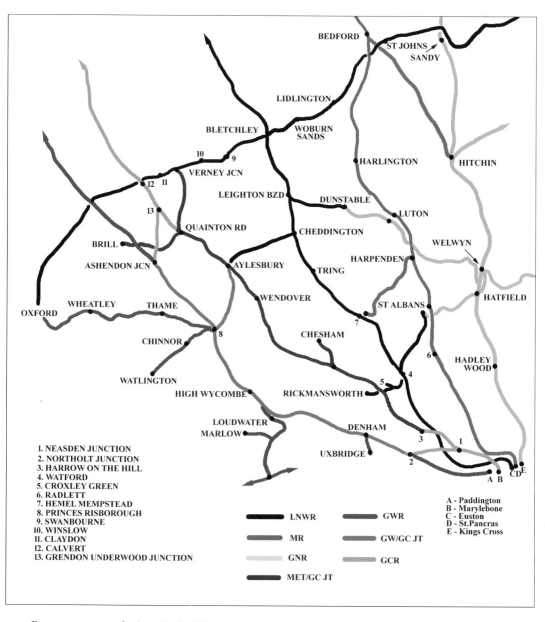

Pre-grouping map of railways in the Chilterns.

The London & North Western Railway

The Premier Line

On 13 July 1957 Jubilee 6P 4-6-0 No. 45674 *Duncan* is in charge of the 15.45 Euston–Manchester London Road. Stanier's Jubilee class was introduced in 1934, a development of Fowler's Patriot class. No. 45674 was built in 1935 and withdrawn in 1964. The gradients on the London & Birmingham Railway were not severe, due mainly to the modest capabilities of early steam locomotives. Nevertheless, the line climbs continuously for 30 miles from Euston to Tring. Here at Hatch End the gradient was 1 in 339. (Photo Ben Brooksbank)

The first station at Watford dates from the opening of the L&B line between Euston and Boxmoor in 1837. A new station 200 yards further south was opened in 1858, at which time Watford became a junction, with the opening of the St Albans branch. The photograph shows a Webb Coal Tank standing in a bay on the west side of the station, presumably waiting to depart with a train for the Rickmansworth branch. These tanks were produced between 1881 and 1887. A total of 300 were built. (Photo courtesy LNWR Society)

To the north of the station are the Watford tunnels. This 1928 view shows the southern portal of the 1-mile 55-yard first tunnel with a 5MT 4-6-0 Black Five on a short passenger train. In 1835, during construction of this tunnel, one of the vertical shafts collapsed killing ten men who were working at the headings. Due to its historic and architectural importance the southern portal is a listed structure.

Seen just outside Kings Langley station in 1945 is what looks like a carefully posed scene. Note that the workman is wearing a tie. The vehicle is LMS 50-ft inspection saloon No. 45028, built at Wolverton in 1942 to diagram 2046. This vehicle has survived into preservation and is presently located at Foxfield waiting restoration. LMS 2P 4-4-0 No. 434 was a Johnson design dating to 1893. It seems incredible that the LMS under Sir Henry Fowler was still building locomotives to this same basic design in 1932. At that time the French, for example, were building compound Pacifics to haul their passenger trains. No. 434 survived until 1956. (Photo courtesy Science Museum)

The 4-4-0 Precursor class was designed by George Whale. 130 were built between 1904 and 1907. They were saturated engines, but a number were later given superheaters, ensuring a longer life than the saturated engines, which were all withdrawn by 1935. At Boxmoor in 1922, superheated No. 1363 *Brindley* is piloting No. 2257 *Vulture*, one of the saturated engines, on an Up Eastbourne express. (Photo courtesy LNWR Society)

On the Up slow at Berkhamstead in October 1950 is Stanier 8F 2-8-0 No. 48257. This locomotive had an interesting history. It was originally built for service with the BEF in France in 1940, but never arrived due to the collapse of France. In 1941 it was shipped out to Iran, seeing service there before being moved to Palestine in 1946. It later saw service with the British Army in the Canal Zone before being returned to Britain in 1949. It was one of the last 8Fs to be withdrawn, meeting its fate in July 1968. (Photo Ben Brooksbank)

Riddles Standard 4MT 2-6-4T No. 80038 heads the 13.10 Euston–Tring past Northchurch. Based largely on Fairburn's 2-6-4T for the LMS, a total of 155 were built, the majority at Brighton. Fifteen have survived into preservation. (Photo Ben Brooksbank)

Until 1987 BR Railfreight was a dedicated railfreight division operating as a single entity, rather than as separate sectors, and mixed freights were a common sight. On the 19 September 1986 Class 85 No. 85010, with No. 85031 dead in tow, heads towards Wembley at Northchurch with a train made up of covered and car transporter wagons. (Photo Peter Lovell)

During the 1980s the West Coast mainline retained a high proportion of locomotive-hauled services. Classes 86–87 dominated passenger services with the older Classes 81–85 on the freight, parcels and some of the lighter passenger work, such as the inter-regionals from the South Coast and the Euston–Northampton semi-fast services. On 16 August 1986 Class 87 No. 87027 heads south near Northchurch with the 11.10 Glasgow Central–Euston. (Photo Peter Lovell)

A hand-coloured lithograph by J. C. Bourne showing the method of construction of the 2½-mile-long Tring Cutting. Wheelbarrows of chalk are being hauled up the wooden barrow runs by horse-driven windlasses. A navvy could lift up to twenty tons of spoil in a day. Altogether 1.5 million tons of Chiltern chalk were removed. The construction of Tring Cutting ruined the contractor Thomas Townshend, who had to file for bankruptcy due to costs far exceeding his estimates.

At Tring station in 1927 George V Class 4-4-0 No. 5384 *S. R. Graves* pilots Claughton 4-6-0 No. 5958 with the Up 'Royal Scot'. The George V Class was introduced in 1910 to the design of Bowen-Cooke. The last were withdrawn in 1948. The Claughtons were another of Bowen-Cooke's designs, being constructed between 1913 and 1921. This was not a very successful design and a number were nominally rebuilt as members of the LMS Patriot class. Just one survived into BR ownership. (Photo courtesy LNWR Society)

H. G. Ivatt's pair of mainline diesel locomotives, Nos 10000 and 10001, made their appearance on the cusp of Nationalisation; No. 10000 in December 1947 and No. 10001 in July 1948. The machines had a Co-Co wheel arrangement and were powered by the English Electric 16SVT, giving a power output of 1600 hp and a top speed of 93 mph. No. 10000 is seen at Tring in October 1950 on a Down mixed freight. A group is currently trying to recreate this locomotive. (Photo Ben Brooksbank)

At about the same time Oliver Bulleid produced three locomotives based on the same English Electric engine. The first of these, No. 10201 is also seen at Tring, this time on an Up fitted freight in 1959. No. 10201 was initially rated at 1,750 hp, later reduced to 1600 hp. Bulleid's locomotives had a 1Co-Co1 wheel arrangement and this type of bogie was also used on BR Classes 40, 44, 45, and 46. (Photo Ben Brooksbank)

In 1923 a gang work on relaying in Tring Cutting. In 1859 the cutting was widened to take three tracks and again in 1876 to take four. Notice the complete lack of safety gear, high viz clothing etc. (Photo courtesy Science Museum)

On 4 July 2019, still in London Midland livery, Unit 350124 stands at Tring having arrived with the 09.04 Euston to Tring. Just discernible are London Northwestern Railway stickers on the windows. This is the brand name for West Midlands Trains services on the Euston route.

On the Up fast line near Cheddington in August 1957 is Royal Scot 7P 4-6-0 No. 46135 *The East Lancashire Regiment* with the 09.45 Blackpool Central to Euston. No. 46135 was originally named *Goliath*. It was renamed in 1934. It was rebuilt from its original parallel boiler form in 1947 and withdrawn in 1962. (Photo Ben Brooksbank)

At Cheddington in full London Northwestern Railway livery is Unit No. 350262, on 4 July 2019, with the 10.19 Rugeley Trent Valley to London Euston via Birmingham New Street. This train runs fast from Leighton Buzzard.

The other passenger operator on the West Coast Main Line is Virgin Trains, which has operated the franchise since 1997. In August 2019 it was announced that the new franchise for long-distance services on the WCML had been awarded to a partnership of First Group and Trenitalia. The franchise, which will run initially until 2026, was due to start on 8 December 2019. At Cheddington, a Class 390 Pendolino passes through the station with the 08.00 Glasgow to Euston. The introduction of the Pendolino trains in 2002 enabled an improvement in journey times due to their ability to run at 125 mph. However, the trains have been heavily criticised for their cramped interiors.

Prior to sectorisation and privatisation very little freight was diesel-hauled on the West Coast mainline. During the 1980s the southern section saw mainly Class 31s on engineering trains and as seen here on 14 August 1987 Class 31 Nos 31161 and 31165 heading south at Soulbury with the King's Cross–Pitstone cement empties, having initially run to Bletchley for the locomotives to run round. (Photo Peter Lovell)

This is the Bletchley station, so well remembered by the author who used to stand by the palings seen in the distance taking down engine numbers. The buildings were designed by J. Livock and completed in 1858. In 1981 the old station buildings were demolished and replaced by a modern design. In the background can be seen the flyover, dating this photograph to post-1961. (Photo courtesy The Science Museum)

One of George Whale's 4-6-0 Experiment class heads away from Bletchley in about 1909 with a Down express. Of note here are the two signal gantries, which carry signals for both directions on the same doll. The circles on the left-hand gantry indicate that they are the signals for the slow lines. (Photo courtesy Science Museum)

A Webb's 5-ft 6-in. 2-4-2 tank No. 6699 stands at the Western side of Bletchley station. This is almost certainly a service for the Buckingham Branch. This line opened in 1850 making Bletchley a four-way junction, the Marston Vale line to Bedford having opened four years earlier. These tanks, introduced in 1890, were very long lived, the last being scrapped in 1955. Note the LNWR ground signal on the left-hand side with its short semaphore arm. (Photo courtesy LNWR Society)

On 29 September 1958 7F Super D 0-8-0 No. 49440 approaches Bletchley station with an Up goods. The Super Ds were a mixture of new builds and locomotives rebuilt from other classes. No. 49440 was one of the new machines. They were strong machines and had a very distinctive exhaust beat. At this time Bletchley Shed had an allocation of nine of these engines. (Photo courtesy RCTS)

A striking photograph of Britannia 4-6-2 No. 70045 *Lord Rowallan* storming through Bletchley with an Up parcels special. At this time No. 70045 was allocated to Holyhead Shed (6J). Notice the co-acting signals. These were a feature of Bletchley at both ends of the station. (Photo courtesy RCTS)

Posed at Bletchley loco shed is Ramsbottom 2-2-2 No. 111 *Russell*, a member of the Problem Class. These locomotives, dating back to a design of 1859, had 7-ft 6-in. driving wheels. Standing in front of the locomotive are the shed cleaners. The photograph dates to a period after 1873, as before this time the engines of this class were cableless. (Photo courtesy LNWR Society)

Bletchley loco shed yard in 1955. The photograph has been taken from beneath the water tower, a favourite spot for loco spotters. In the foreground is Stanier 2-6-4T No. 42582. Also seen are a 4F 0-6-0 Jinty and a Stanier 8F 2-8-0. At this time Bletchley would have had an allocation of about sixty locomotives. (Photo Lamberhurst)

The date is 5 July 1965 and the last steam locomotive, Stanier 8F 2-8-0 No. 48610, is about to leave Bletchley shed. Gathered in front of the locomotive is the shed staff. The author had two uncles and a grandfather who worked at Bletchley. One of the uncles, Tom Parker, stands third from the left, bottom tier.

Denbigh Hall Bridge, the furthest extent of the L&BR, on 9 April 1838. A plaque on the bridge commemorates this fact. Passengers were conveyed by coach until the intervening section to Rugby was opened on 17 September. Notice the Up and Down signals on the same post. The signal box is Denbigh Hall. The road under the bridge is Watling Street, later the A5. (Photo courtesy Science Museum)

The Aylesbury Branch

The importance of the town of Aylesbury is reflected in the fact that even before the L&BR had completed its main line, in 1836 a branch from Cheddington was authorised and opened just over a year after the main line. The initial service was of three trains on weekdays and two on Sundays. By 1895 there were ten services on weekdays with a journey time of eighteen minutes. In 1860 the intermediate station of Marston Gate appeared in public timetables for the first time. After the Second World War decline set in and the line closed to passengers in February 1953 and to goods traffic in December of the same year. Just two days before final closure to passengers Webb 5-ft 6-in. 2-4-2T No. 46601 stands at the branch platform at Cheddington with a service for Aylesbury. (Photo Ben Brooksbank)

The Oxford to Cambridge Line

The Bedford Railway opened in 1846. Until the arrival of the Leicester to Hitchin line in 1857, giving access to King's Cross, the people of Bedford had to travel to Bletchley to reach London, or anywhere else for that matter. In 1868 the Midland extension to St Pancras opened, diminishing traffic on both the other routes. The Bedford–Bletchley line was worked by the LNWR from the outset and absorbed by that company in 1879. The station at Bedford was at St Johns, seen in this 1962 view. (Photo Lamberhurst)

Five years later a Derby Lightweight unit waits at Bedford St Johns with a service for Oxford. Notice the yellow diamond coupling code, which meant these units could only be coupled with units bearing the same code. In 1984 the station was relocated further north in the former goods yard. This has enabled trains on the Marston valley line to terminate at Bedford Midland. (Photo Geoffrey Skelsey)

The Bedford & Cambridge Railway opened in 1862. It absorbed the earlier (1857) Sandy & Potton Railway. It was worked by and later became part of the LNWR. Complete closure came on 1 January 1968. Two years before closure, the signalman of Bedford St Johns No. 2 signal box leans out to collect the token from the driver of a Derby Lightweight unit arriving from the Cambridge direction. None of these Lightweight units remained in service after 1969. (Photo courtesy RCTS)

Lidlington was one of the original stations on the line, opening on 18 November 1846. On 5 July 1991 a Class 108 unit arrives with the 17.50 Bletchley to Bedford service. Considerable changes have taken place since this photograph was taken. The signal cabin and crossing gates have gone, to be replaced by automatic barriers, and the Up platform is now on the other side of the crossing.

Aspley Guise was one of seven new halts opened in October 1905. It was closed between 1917 and 1919. It is another station which has seen considerable change. The crossing gates and crossing keeper's cabin have gone to be replaced by automatic barriers. The Up platform has been located to the other side of the crossing. On 31 July 1989 No. 31456 passes through with a train of ballast destined for the Forder's Siding refuse tip.

Woburn Sands was another of the original stations opened in 1846. It was originally named just Woburn, the name change coming in 1860. Several stations were built in this *cottage orné* style, so beloved of the Victorians. The signal box was abolished in 2004, along with the others on the line, which is now controlled from the Marston Vale Signalling Centre. On 31 July 1989 a Class 108 DMU arrives with a Bletchley–Bedford service.

Vivarail unit No. 230003 approaches Bow Brickhill station with a Bletchley–Bedford working on 1 July 2019. These units have been rebuilt from London Underground D78 stock. The unit is powered by two Ford Duratorq five-cylinder engines rated at 185 hp on each driving car. A Class 37 running light engine retreats into the distance.

Approaching Bletchley station on the Down slow is 4F 0-6-0 No. 43977 with a Class H freight train on 11 April 1963. No. 43977 had just another seven months left in service before being withdrawn. In the background is the famous Bletchley Flyover. This gigantic structure crossed from the Oxford Line to a point to the east of the main lines where it then divided, one line going to the WCML and the other to the Cambridge Line. The idea was that the Oxford–Cambridge Line would become a major freight route and the flyover would avoid the need for trains to cross the layout at Bletchley. Work started in 1959 and was completed in 1962. Unfortunately, events overtook these plans and the flyover was very little used. However, it may one day come into its own as it will form part of the East–West Rail Project and it is proposed that a station will be built on the flyover itself. (Photo Ben Brooksbank)

As part of the plan for the east–west freight route, which included the Bletchley Flyover, the sidings at Swanbourne were to be developed into a major marshalling yard, and land was bought for this purpose. The sidings that already existed were opened during the Second World War. The development never happened, and the existing sidings were closed in 1967. When this photograph was taken in April 1990 the line was still in use for freight traffic, but passenger traffic had ceased in 1968.

The Buckingham Railway opened the line from Bletchley to Banbury in May 1850 with the line from Verney Junction to Oxford being completed in May 1851. Winslow became an important station as it was here that trains for Banbury and Oxford divided or joined. Along with the other stations on the Bletchley–Oxford line Winslow closed in 1968. However, shoppers' specials continued to run until 1985. In the 1960s a Derby Lightweight unit has stopped at Winslow with a service for Oxford. (Photo courtesy RCTS)

Before Verney Junction station was built in 1868 this spot was known as Claydon Junction. This is a view west in 1966, with a Derby Lightweight unit ready to depart for Oxford. The lines leading away to the right are to Buckingham and Banbury; closed to passengers in 1964 and 1961 respectively. Verney Junction is named after Sir Harry Verney one of the promoters of the Buckingham Railway. It could be said that he had three stations named for him, since his previous name was Calvert and his house was named Claydon. (Photo courtesy RCTS)

A view in the other direction at Verney Junction taken at the same period. The lines on the right were previously used by trains coming from the GC/Met Joint line from Quainton Road and Aylesbury. That line closed completely in 1947. It turned away from the Oxford–Cambridge line at the far end of the line of carriages. No buildings now remain here, just a pair of overgrown platforms. (Photo Lamberhurst)

Claydon station opened on 1 May 1850. In 1966 a Class 24 approaches from the west with a mixed freight. Class 24 was the predecessor of the more powerful Class 25. All were withdrawn by 1980. To the west of Claydon is Claydon LNE Junction, a July 1940 addition to enable access to the GC/Met Joint line. Everything seen in this photograph has been obliterated. (Photo courtesy RCTS)

Launton station opened on 1 October 1850. It closed along with the rest of the stations on this section of line in 1968. The line remained open for freight and special trains. The very last train to traverse the line was Hertfordshire Railtours 'The Mothball'. Hauled by Class 56 No. 56046, the train is seen passing through Launton on 23 May 1993.

The Oxford to Bicester section of the Oxford–Bletchley line was completely rebuilt to modern standards during 2014/2015 to enable through Marylebone–Oxford services to operate via the chord between Bicester Gavray and Bicester South Junctions. A number of crossings have been eliminated and at Oddington-on-Otmoor the crossing has been replaced by a large bridge that has proved a convenient vantage point for photographers. On 7 March 2016 Class 168 No. 168108 heads towards Islip with the 10.05 Marylebone–Oxford Parkway. At this stage of the work Oxford North Junction was still being rebuilt and services were terminating at Oxford Parkway. (Photo Peter Lovell)

Rebuilding of the section around Oxford North Junction in 2016 meant that the Whatley Quarry–Oxford Banbury Road stone trains could not take the direct route via Didcot, Swindon and Westbury. Instead the traffic came up to Acton Yard and was then tripped to Banbury Road via High Wycombe and the Bicester Chord. On 28 November 2016 Class 59 No. 59104 approaches Oddington Bridge with the 11.04 Oxford Banbury Road–Acton empties. (Photo Peter Lovell)

The Leighton Buzzard to Dunstable Branch

In LMS days Watford tank No. 6917 stands in the branch platform at Leighton Buzzard with a train for the Dunstable Branch. The name Watford derives from the fact that they were at one time commonly used on Euston–Watford trains. They were more officially known as 18-inch or 5-ft 3-in. tanks. No. 6917 survived into BR ownership but never had its number of No. 46917 actually applied, being withdrawn in April 1949. (Photo courtesy LNWR Society)

Also setting off for the Dunstable Branch, brake van in tow, is Bletchley engine Super D No. 49403. These hard-slogging engines were well suited to the branch with its 1 in 40 Sewell Bank. The gradient here was originally intended to be 1 in 27 and would have been a rope-worked incline. The 6¾-mile line, engineered by George Stephenson, opened on 1 June 1848. By 1890 there were nine trains a day completing the journey in fifteen minutes. (Photo Lamberhurst)

Stanbridgeford was the only intermediate station between Leighton and Dunstable North. This was an extremely popular stop for people visiting the nearby Totternhoe Knolls. Standing in the station on 27 August 1932 is a Webb Coal Tank. (Photo courtesy LNWR Society)

There were a number of industrial branches on the line. Vauxhall Motors used the line until 1981 and the Dunstable Oil Terminal was in use until 1990. At Totternhoe was the Rugby Portland Cement Company, which had its own locomotives. Seen here is No. 8, one of the company's Sentinel 4W 100 hp single engine locomotives, shunting wagons at the works. These wagons will be hauled up the 1 in 10 rope-worked incline to the BR exchange sidings. The company ceased using rail transport in 1965.

Dunstable APCM (Blue Circle) at Houghton Regis also had its own locomotives. Two of their fleet are seen here on 19 June 1954. On the right is 0-4-0ST *Tom Parry* (Andrew Barclay No. 2015 of 1935) and 0-4-0ST *Punch Hill* (Andrew Barclay No. 776 of 1896). Production of cement stopped in 1971 but the site continued as a rail served depot until 1990. (Photo courtesy RCTS)

Nearly the end. Passenger traffic between Dunstable North and Leighton Buzzard ceased on 2 July 1962 but Dunstable North remained open for passenger services towards Luton and Hatfield. These services continued until 26 April 1965. A Class 105 Cravens unit stands at Dunstable North with a service to Hatfield on 29 March 1965.

The St Albans Branch

The first station in St Albans was opened by the LNWR on 5 May 1858 at the end of a branch from Watford. This 6½-mile line had intermediate stations at Bricket Wood and Park Street. Callowland, later renamed Watford North, followed in 1910, Garston in 1966, and How Wood in 1988. St Albans was renamed St Albans Abbey in 1924 and the line was electrified in 1988. In 1895 there were fifteen trains per day on weekdays, with a journey time of fifteen minutes. For most of the Up trains the two intermediate stations were request stops. Today (2019) there are twenty-two services during the week with a journey time of sixteen minutes. Services are operated by a Class 319 unit. The line was proposed for closure in the Beeching Report but happily survived. In 1937 Webb 2-4-2T 5-ft 6-in. tank No. 6729 waits to leave St Albans with a train for Watford. (Photo courtesy LNWR Society)

The Rickmansworth Branch

On 15 September 1962 a Class 501 EMU is seen at Croxley Green; terminus of the branch on the former Rickmansworth Line. This line was the conception of Lord Ebury, who wished to connect Watford with the GWR's Uxbridge station. Lack of funds meant that the line got only as far as Rickmansworth. Services on the 4½-mile branch, which started on 1 October 1862, were operated by the LNWR, which took over the line completely in 1881. In 1895 the ten-minute journey cost fourpence in third class. Rickmansworth station was renamed Rickmansworth Church Street in 1950, and in March 1952 passenger services were withdrawn. Freight services continued until 1967. (Photo courtesy RCTS)

The intermediate station on the Croxley Branch was Watford West, seen here under construction in 1912. The Croxley Branch remained open until 1996. At that time the line was breached by a new road and bus services were substituted. This state of affairs continued until 2003 when the bus services were withdrawn. Work started on the Croxley Rail Link, a scheme to join the Croxley Branch with the Metropolitan Line's Croxley station, thus completing the link between Rickmansworth and Watford. However this project has now stalled and is unlikely to resume any time in the near future.

The Great Northern Railway

The Great Northern Main Line

The original temporary GNR terminus in London was at Maiden Lane. This was opened in 1850. King's Cross station, designed by Lewis Cubitt, came into operation on 14 October 1852. There were just two platforms, today's platforms 1 and 8. The space in between was used for carriage sidings. The suburban platforms on the west side of the station were added in 1875. King's Cross is currently used by London North Eastern Railway, Hull Trains, Grand Central, Thameslink, and Great Northern. Thameslink and Great Northern are both part of Govia Thameslink Railway.

In 1944 Edward Thompson ordered the construction of thirty Pacifics based on the A2/2 design, itself a rebuild of Gresley's P2. Only fifteen were actually built to Thompson's design, designated A2/3. No. 60523 *Sun Castle* is seen here north of Wood Green with a Down Leeds train. In the background a Cravens Class 105 DMU takes the flyover on to the Hertford Loop line. The Loop line was built to both relieve congestion caused by the Welwyn bottleneck and to serve new suburban stations. Although authorised in 1898 it was not completed until 1924. (Photo Peter Groom)

Gresley V2 2-6-2 No. 60862 emerges from the 705-yard Wood Green tunnel on the Down fast with a Class C express freight on 15 June 1962. The V2s were introduced in 1936 and a total of 184 were built between then and 1944. Problems with the monobloc cylinder casting led to a number of engines having the casting replaced by separate cylinders, as here with No. 60862. This engine was one of only eight of the class which was fitted with a double chimney. It is here at Wood Green that the real climbing begins with 8 miles at 1 in 200 to Potters Bar, the summit of the first of the Chiltern Hills to be encountered. (Photo Peter Groom)

In the late 1920s six of Robinson's A5 4-6-2Ts were transferred from Bradford to King's Cross to work services to Hitchin and Baldock. Here we see A5 No. 5452 approaching Greenwood signal box on the Down fast with a train of six-wheelers. As BR No. 69812 this engine was withdrawn from 40E Colwick in 1959. After Greenwood box the four tracks became two through Hadley Wood tunnel. This section was widened in the late 1950s, the work included building a second Hadley Wood tunnel.

In June 1959 Thompson B1 4-6-0 No. 61406 pounds up the gradient at Hadley Wood with a train for Cleethorpes. The B1s were robust workhorses, as is evidenced by its eleven-coach load. Introduced in 1942, a total of 410 B1s were built, the last entering service in 1952. A number were named after antelopes, including No. 8306 *Bongo*. Ever after, the class was unofficially known as 'Bongos'. (Photo Peter Groom)

Relegated to more humble duties is Gresley A3 4-6-2 Pacific No. 60044 *Melton*, seen leaving Potters Bar with the 19.23 King's Cross to Peterborough on 10 June 1963. This is probably the last photograph taken of No. 60044 in action as the engine was withdrawn from 34A King's Cross just six days later. (Photo courtesy RCTS)

When introduced in 1995 the Class 365 EMU was conceived as a dual voltage unit, and indeed equipped with both 25 kV AC and 750 V DC equipment. However, the units were never actually used on DC lines. Starting in 2014 the fleet underwent an extensive refurbishment programme. Currently the trains are used on Great Northern services from King's Cross to Peterborough and to Cambridge/Ely. On 6 July 2019 the 09.04 Peterborough to King's Cross service approaches Welham Green on the Up fast. Welham Green is a new station opened on 29 September 1986. It has platforms only on the slow lines.

A view of Hatfield station in the early twentieth century. The freight train is on the Up fast. Hatfield retains this staggered platform layout to this day. The station was an important junction, with branches to St Albans, to Hertford, and to Dunstable. The next station north of Hatfield was Three Counties, named after the nearby asylum. It opened in 1866 with the name Arlesey Siding and closed in 1959.

On a Down semi-fast service is Thompson A2/3 4-6-2 Pacific No. 60520 *Owen Tudor*, seen on 14 May 1959 leaving Hatfield station. Note that the rolling stock consists exclusively of pre-Nationalisation vehicles. In 1957 No. 60520 was involved in a serious accident near Welwyn Garden City, when it ran into the back of a local train in fog, while hauling the 19.10 Aberdeen to King's Cross express. One person was killed. No. 60520 had a short working life, emerging from Doncaster Works in 1947 and being withdrawn in June 1963. No examples of Thompson Pacifics survived into preservation. The lines seen here from right to left are: Down and Up Dunstable, Down slow, Down fast, Up fast, Up slow, Up goods, London Road Siding. Today just the two fast lines and the two slow lines remain. (Photo Peter Groom)

Welwyn Garden City station opened in 1926. Until that time there had just been the Welwyn Garden City Halt on the Hatfield–Dunstable line. The new station had four platform lines as well as the two through fast lines. It was opened by Neville Chamberlain. On 15 June 1935 there was a serious accident at the station. This was caused by the signalman accepting a second train when the first was still in section. The second train ran into the rear of the first at speed and fourteen people died. As a result of this accident, a new system was put in place on the LNER, and generally on Britain's Railways, which made it impossible to accept a second train into an occupied section. This is known as a Welwyn Control.

At Welwyn the challenge of the Chiltern Hills is overcome by means of the two Welwyn tunnels; Welwyn North at 1,046 yards and Welwyn South at 446 yards. The line climbs through the tunnels to reach a summit beyond Woolmer Green. On 2 June 1951 Gresley A4 4-6-2 No. 60028 *Walter K. Whigham* emerges from Welwyn North tunnel with the 12.15 Newcastle to King's Cross. Walter Whigham was the deputy chairman of the LNER. No. 60028, then carrying the number 4487, was originally named *Sea Eagle*. It received its new name in 1947. (Photo Ben Brooksbank)

Nearly thirty years later, in September 1980, Class 40 No. 40003 emerges from the same tunnel with a special working. No. 40003, then numbered D203, was one of the original ten pilot scheme English Electric type 4 locomotives ordered as part of the Modernisation Plan and emerged from the Vulcan Foundry in 1958. The Class 40 was not entirely successful and was considered to be underpowered but achieved a considerable following amongst enthusiasts, so much so that seven of the class have been preserved. No. 40003 was not among them and was withdrawn in 1982.

On the same day an unidentified Class 47 is seen between the two tunnels with a northbound service. The photograph was taken from the south portal of Welwyn North tunnel. The two tunnels are separated by just 286 yards. The contractor for the line and the tunnels was Thomas Brassey. Both line and tunnels were completed in 1850. There have been a number of plans over the years to eliminate the Welwyn bottleneck, which consists of Digswell Viaduct, the two tunnels and Welwyn North station but to date nothing has actually been done.

Knebworth station was not one of the original stations on the line, not opening until February 1884. It has platforms on all four lines, but the two fast line platforms are normally fenced off out of use. On 29 June 2019 DB Cargo UK EMD Class 66 No. 66128 passes through Knebworth on the Down slow with an engineering train. The Class 66 has a 139.2 litre 2-stroke V12 engine giving 3,300 hp.

A nice study of V2 2-6-2 No. 60983 passing Hitchin with the Up Scarborough Flyer on 2 July 1960. The signal box is Hitchin South. On the right is the engineer's yard. The LNER launched the Scarborough Flyer in 1927. With a break between 1939 and 1950 it then continued until 1963. (Photo courtesy RCTS)

At Hitchin in 1955 the auto-train to Bedford is about to depart, being propelled by Ivatt 2MT 2-6-2T No. 41270. The Ivatt tanks were introduced in 1946. Ten were built by the LMS and a further 120 by BR. Fifty were push-pull fitted. The signal box is Hitchin Yard. (Photo Ben Brooksbank)

The Bedford–Hitchin line had long been in decline but was sustained to some extent by special trains for servicemen from Henlow Camp. Standing at the Down platform at Hitchin on 16 March 1957 is one of these trains, consisting of Holden J15 0-6-0 No. 65479 and two sets of Gresley quad-art carriages. The J15s were very successful locomotives. The basic design dates back to 1883 and they continued to be built until 1913. The last was not withdrawn until 1962. No. 65462 has survived into preservation. (Photo Ben Brooksbank)

English Electric type 2 No. D5900 stands at Hitchin with an Up local train on 30 March 1961. These 'Baby Deltics' were powered by a 1,160 hp Napier Deltic T9-29 diesel engine, the same engine two of which equipped the Class 55 Deltics. 'The Baby Deltics' were later rebuilt with a different front end, losing the connecting doors and having the headcode discs replaced by a headcode box. These machines were not a great success and being non-standard all were withdrawn within ten years. Somewhat incredibly, there is a project currently underway to build a replica 'Baby Deltic' based on a Deltic engine in a modified Class 37 body. (Photo Ben Brooksbank)

The old order still giving faithful service after more than forty years. Leading HST power car No. 43290 blasts through Hitchin with 1E07, the 08.30 Edinburgh to King's Cross on 17 July 2019. The High-Speed Train was introduced in 1976 and had a transformative effect on Great Western, Great Northern, and, later, Midland express services. The power cars have been re-engined several times. No. 43290 is fitted with the 76.3 litre MTU 16V 4000 RVI engine and appropriately enough is named *MTU Fascination of Power*.

The new order. A few minutes later a Class 800/1 Azuma unit passes with train 1A25 the 10.45 Leeds–King's Cross service. LNER has ordered thirteen Class 800/1 nine-car sets and ten Class 800/2 five-car sets. These are bi-mode trains and are equipped with the 21 litre MTU 12V 1600 R80L diesel engine. Class 800/1 has five of these under-floor mounted power packs while Class 800/2 has three. The trains will operate at 125 mph but are capable of 140 mph using ETCS. LNER will also receive twelve Class 801/1 and thirty Class 801/2 electric units. These units will each be equipped with one 'last mile' MTU power pack.

A rare colour photograph taken at Hitchin loco shed in about 1937. On the left is Class C1 Ivatt Large Atlantic 4-4-2 No. 3272, built in 1904. On the right is Ivatt D2 4-4-0 No. 4337, built in 1889. At the time, both of these were Hitchin engines and neither survived to carry a BR number. No. 3272 was withdrawn in 1947, with No. 4337 following the year after. The latter was allocated the BR number 62163 but never carried it. Hitchin shed opened with the railway in 1850 and closed to steam in 1961, although it continued to have an allocation of diesels for a few years thereafter. Under BR it was 34D and later HI. There was also a Midland Railway shed at Hitchin. This opened in 1875 and closed in 1920. (Photo courtesy RCTS)

Arlesy and Shefford (note spelling) opened with the railway in 1850. It became Arlesey and Shefford Road in 1860 and for a short period in the late nineteenth century it was simply Arlesey. In 1933 it was renamed Arlesey and Henlow. It was closed by BR in 1959 and the buildings subsequently demolished. A newly built 'Arlesey' station was opened in October 1988. There are only platforms on the slow lines and facilities consist of a booking office and waiting area and the usual platform 'bus shelters'. Heading south on 29 June 2019 is an InterCity 225 set. These trains which, consist of a Class 91 locomotive, nine carriages and a driving trailer, were introduced for the ECML electrification in 1989.

On 7 August 1960 A3 Pacific No. 60049 *Galtee More* is seen just after leaving Sandy with the 16.57 King's Cross to Grantham. On the far left is the line from Bedford, part of the Oxford–Cambridge line. This line crossed the ECML on a flyover a little further to the north. It ran parallel to the main line to the LMS station south of that of the LNER, before curving away from the mainline towards Cambridge. No. 60049 was a 35B Grantham engine at this time and survived just another two years before being withdrawn at the end of 1962. (Photo courtesy RCTS)

The Hertford, Luton & Dunstable Railway

The Hertford & Welwyn Junction Railway was formed in 1853 and its line opened in March 1858. The station at Hertford, seen here, was usually known as Cowbridge. Trains ran to Welwyn Junction station on the GNR main line, but this station remained open only until 1860, after which trains ran to Hatfield. In 1876 a line parallel to the main line was completed and trains from Hertford used this to reach Hatfield and the junction at Welwyn was removed. When the GNR's Hertford Loop was completed in 1924, services were transferred to the new Hertford North station, although Cowbridge remained open for freight.

There were just two intermediate stations, Hertingfordbury and Cole Green. This is Hertingfordbury, seen in 1963 after the line had closed to all traffic the previous year. The station looks as remote as it actually was, some distance from the tiny community it served. Attimore Hall and Hatfield Hyde Halts opened in May 1905 but were not successful and closed almost immediately, although Attimore Hall remained open for freight. (Photo Lamberhurst)

Cole Green served an equally small community. In a photograph taken probably near the end of the nineteenth century, Stirling G2 0-4-4BT No. 531 stands at the head of a train bound for Hertford. Passenger services were initially provided jointly by the GNR and the Eastern Counties Railway. By the time this photograph was taken the GNR was providing twelve or thirteen services a day between Hertford and Hatfield. Passenger services ceased in 1951 while freight continued until 1962.

As late as 1939 the LNER were still providing eight or nine services per weekday. In that era, ex-GCR 0-6-2T No. 5535 is seen near Hatfield with a Hertford–King's Cross working. This Parker-designed locomotive was very long lived, having been built in 1894, it was not withdrawn until 1960, one of the very last survivors of the class.

Welwyn Garden City Halt was a late arrival on the scene, opening in 1920 on the Hatfield Dunstable line just where it curved away from the GNR line. When the main line station opened in 1926 the halt closed.

This view of the main lines shows the Dunstable line curving away to the left. The sign 'BRANCH REDUCE SPEED FOR CURVE' applies to the Hertford line which curves away to the right a further two hundred yards or so to the north.

While the H&WJR was getting itself built the Luton Dunstable & Welwyn Junction Railway was struggling to build its line. In 1858 a merger of the two companies was authorised, the merged railway becoming the Hertford Luton & Dunstable Railway. The line between Luton and Welwyn was completed in 1860, at which time Welwyn Junction station was closed and trains from the Luton line also ran to Hatfield. In 1861 the railway became part of the GNR. Ayot was not one of the original stations on the line. It opened as Ayott St Peter in 1877. In 1948 it was destroyed by fire and subsequently closed to passengers, although it remained open for freight.

A view of Wheathampstead in the early twentieth century as a Luton-bound train arrives. Unlike Ayot, Wheathamstead did not have a passing loop, hence the single platform. The station's most famous passenger was George Bernard Shaw, who lived at nearby Ayot St Lawrence. The station along with the others on the line closed to passengers in 1965.

On 17 April 1965, at Harpenden East, a Class 105 Cravens unit waits to depart with the 14.21 SO Dunstable to Hatfield service. This was just nine days before the line closed to passenger traffic. The Cravens units were particularly associated with the Eastern Region, especially in the early years. A total of 302 cars was constructed. The last units were withdrawn in 1988. Between Harpenden East (the East was added in 1950 to distinguish it from Harpenden on the Midland Main Line) and Luton Hoo the HLDR passed under the MML. There was no connection between the two lines until January 1966 when a junction was put in to enable trains from the MML to reach the freight facilities at Dunstable. (Photo courtesy RCTS)

Luton Bute Street station was adjacent to Luton Midland Road, the MR station. On 19 September 1964 Fowler 4F 0-6-0 No. 44414 leaves the station with South Bedfordshire Locomotive Club's 'The Cobbler', a railtour which included Wellingborough, Newport Pagnell and Northampton.

The trackbed of the HL&DR between Luton and Dunstable was turned into a guided busway in 2013. This is the Luton end of the busway. Between Luton and Dunstable was the station of Chaul End. This opened in 1915 and closed again in 1919. It never appeared in the public timetable.

The first section of the HL&DR to be completed was between Luton and Dunstable, which opened to freight on 5 April 1858, and to passengers on the following 3 May. Originally known as Dunstable Church Street, the station became Dunstable Town in 1927. In 1955 there were five trains on weekdays from Dunstable to Hatfield, one continuing through to King's Cross. These trains started back at Dunstable North, the former LNW station. There were also a number of trains from Dunstable North to Luton only. In the reverse direction there were only three trains. Passengers for the most part had to change at Luton to reach Dunstable.

The Hatfield to St Albans Branch

The Hatfield & St Albans Railway received its Act in 1862 and opened its line on 16 October 1865. It was worked from the outset by the GNR, which eventually absorbed the H&StAR in November 1883. The GNR had running powers into the LNWR station but it also had its own station at London Road. The photograph was taken in 1992 when the building and yard were in use by a scrap dealer. The station building, which is listed, is now a business centre and sits in the middle of a new housing estate.

There was an intermediate station, Springfield, which was renamed Smallford in 1879. The railway was soon in trouble. In 1868 the Midland Railway's main line was completed and with it came St Alban's City station, which took away much of the business and led to its eventual absorption by the GNR.

In 1899 Hill End station opened to serve the Herts County Mental Hospital. The hospital had its own siding. In 1897 the Salvation Army Halt came into being. This was for the workers at the Salvation Army's Campsfield Printing Works. The organisation also had its own siding for despatching its printed material. At the Salvation Army Halt, Stirling G2 0-4-4BT, with the curious number of 116A, is shunting wagons.

Nast Hyde Halt was opened in 1910. In 1939, at the outbreak of war, services on the line were suspended. However, they were soon reinstated to enable workers to travel to the De Havilland aircraft factory at Hatfield. Lemford Road Halt was opened in 1942 for this purpose, although it never appeared in public timetables. (Photo Lamberhurst)

This is the Midland Railway bridge just near London Road station. It was the Midland that mostly did for the GNR branch. Passenger services were withdrawn on 28 September 1951. The last train was hauled by N7/1 No. 69644. Freight continued and the scrapyard at Smallford was serviced by rail up to 1969, the year of final closure.

The Midland Railway

The Midland Main Line

St Pancras station was undoubtedly the crowning glory of the Midland Railway. It was designed by William Barlow, the MR engineer. The station was built over a cellar, which was used to store beer barrels coming down from Burton. This is the space where Eurostar travellers now wait for their trains. The ironwork for the 240-ft wide and 100-ft high roof was manufactured by the Butterley Company. The station was opened in October 1868. The Midland Hotel which fronts the station was designed by Sir Gilbert Scott. This view dates from 1947, the last year of the LMS. Note particularly the huge piles of parcels and other goods on either side of the station; traffic which has now completely disappeared. (Photo courtesy Science Museum)

Difficult to believe this is the same station, were it not for that magnificent roof. These are the Eurostar platforms, which occupy the same space as seen in the 1947 photograph.

An unidentified LMS Garratt 2-6-0 + 0-6-2T hauls a long Toton–Brent Yard coal train through Elstree and Borehamwood station on 27 March 1954. The Garratts were built between 1927 and 1930, the majority later being fitted with rotary bunkers, as seen here. The Garratts suffered from that recurring MR problem of inadequate axleboxes, causing frequent overheating. The whole class was withdrawn by 1958. (Photo Ben Brooksbank)

In May 1937 Johnson 3P 4-4-0 No. 707 heads away from Elstree on the Up fast with a collection of postal vehicles. This class of eighty engines were the first MR locomotives to be fitted with Belpaire fireboxes and were consequently known as 'Belpaires'. The tracks divide here in order to pass through the Elstree tunnels. The second tunnel was completed in 1895 at the time of the quadrupling of the line. (Photo courtesy RCTS)

Fowler 3MT 2-6-2 No. 40022 is seen on the Down slow at Radlett on 30 August 1958 with the 17.20 St Pancras to St Albans. At this time the journey would have taken forty-five minutes or more, depending on the stopping pattern. A small acceleration came in 1960 with the introduction of Class 127 diesel multiple units, journeys now taking thirty to thirty-eight minutes. No. 40022 was the last of its class to survive, being withdrawn from Cricklewood East in 1962. (Photo Ben Brooksbank)

Shortly after passing through Radlett station Class 45 Peak No. D41 is seen in August 1966 with a train from Leeds to St Pancras. The Peaks were introduced in 1960 and were particularly associated with the Midland Main Line. North of Radlett was Napsbury station, opened in 1905 with just an island platform on the slow lines. It had a branch to the Middlesex County Asylum. Just north of the station the main line was joined by a branch from Park Street on the LNW St Alban's Abbey branch. This goods-only line was opened by the MR in 1866 for use during the construction of the Bedford to London extension. By the 1890s it was out of use. (Photo Peter Groom)

The Thameslink network was inaugurated in 1988 using the newly built Class 319 units. In this view First Capital Connect unit No. 319006 is leaving St Albans City on 5 April 2014 with a Thameslink service via Sutton. The arrival of newer units has seen the Class 319 units transferred to other regions. A number will be converted to Class 769 dual mode units. (Photo Matt Buck)

North of Harpenden was Chiltern Green station. The GNR Hatfield–Luton–Dunstable line crossed just south of here then ran alongside the MML to reach its own station of Luton Hoo. The tiny hamlet of New Mill End, where the two stations were located, was unable to sustain two stations and Chiltern Green closed in 1952. Luton station opened with the London extension in 1868. It was originally known as Luton Midland Road to distinguish it from the nearby GNR Luton Bute Street station. Until the mid-1980s the main line services on the MML were in the hands of the Class 45 Peaks. On 26 March 1981 Peak No. 45134 departs from Luton with a Down express. (Photo Barry Lewis)

The Peaks were replaced with InterCity 125 units (HSTs). Since 2004 the HSTs have been supplemented by Class 222 Meridians. These multiple units operate in various formations. Each vehicle is powered by a six-cylinder 19 litre Cummins QSK19 diesel engine rated at 750 hp. On 17 July 2019 East Midland Trains No. 222009 arrives at Luton with the 09.32 Corby to St Pancras.

Yet another in the long procession of coal trains heading for London, this time in the hands of BR Standard 9F 2-10-0 No. 92015 as it passes through Leagrave station in April 1955. At Luton and Leagrave the MML passes through something of a gap in the Chilterns. Nevertheless, there is still a long climb from Bedford and the enginemen will have been working hard on the 17-mile climb with gradients at up to 1 in 200. (Photo Ben Brooksbank)

A lot easier work for Class 45 Peak No. D134 as it passes through the cutting north of Leagrave with the 10.00 Manchester Central to St Pancras on 26 June 1965. The chalk of the Chiltern Hills is very evident in this photograph. When the railway was built Leagrave was a hamlet in remote countryside. Today it is a suburb of Luton. (Photo courtesy RCTS)

The LMS 5P4F 2-6-0 Crab was designed by George Hughes and was essentially a L&Y design. Henry Fowler insisted on the fitting of a number of Derby standard components, including the tender, which being narrower than the cab, gave the locomotive an odd appearance. The success of the design is attested to by the fact that the last of the class was not withdrawn until 1967, having been built in 1927. On 9 April 1955 No. 42839 rumbles along the Up slow at Harlington with a Class E freight. (Photo Ben Brooksbank)

Harlington station opened at the same time as the others on the London extension. From being a remote country station at opening, it is now a commuter hub. To cope with the phenomenal success of the Thameslink network, a fleet of new trains was ordered in 2010 and entered service from 2016. This is the Class 700 Desiro City, delivered in fixed formations of eight or twelve cars. On 2 July 2019 No. 700109, one of the twelve vehicle units, arrives at Harlington with the 13.19 Bedford to Brighton.

Somewhat unusually, Class 45 Peak No. 45108 has been put on to the Up slow just north of Ampthill Tunnel with an express from the north. The Peaks, the mainstay of express services at this time, were equipped with the Sulzer 12LDA28B, a twelve-cylinder twin-bank engine of 264 litres, giving 2,500 hp. No. 45108 has survived into preservation. The photograph dates from 31 August 1980.

On the same day another southbound express is more appropriately on the Up fast behind Peak No. 45126. The overhead electrification is already in place at this location but electric services between Bedford and St Pancras did not start until 1983.

Near the location of the former Ampthill station Class 25 Sulzer type 2 No. 25141 heads north with an electrification train in August 1980. Ampthill station closed in 1959 and there is an ongoing campaign, so far unsuccessful, for it to reopen. One campaign that does seem to be having more success is for a new station at Wixams, south of Bedford, near a large new housing development. The precise location of the new station has yet to be decided.

At Millbrook is an unusual working as a pair of Class 28 Co-Bos, Nos D5703 and D5710, head the 10.25 Manchester Central to St Pancras. These Metropolitan-Vickers machines were equipped with a two-stroke Crossley HST V8 engine giving 1,200 hp. Two-stroke engines were very unusual in British diesel locomotive practice although common practice in North American-built machines. The Co-Bos were notoriously unreliable, and none lasted longer than ten years in service. (Photo Ben Brooksbank)

The Midland Railway's station at Bedford came into existence with the opening of the MR line from Leicester to Hitchin in 1858, which gave the company access to London via the GNR line to King's Cross. The inhabitants of Bedford were more than happy as prior to this time they had to travel via the Marston Vale line to Bletchley and change there for Euston. The photograph shows Standard 4MT 4-6-0 No. 75055 at Bedford with the RCTS Northern and Eastern tour on 10 August 1958. This is the original station. The present station, 110 yards to the north, was opened in 1978. (Photo Ben Brooksbank)

Standing at Bedford is Fowler 3MT 2-6-2T No. 40026 dating from 1931. Like a number of others in the class it was equipped for push-pull working and also had condensing apparatus. At the time the photograph was taken in July 1960 it was a Bedford engine. It moved to Kentish Town in 1962 and was scrapped the same year. (Photo courtesy RCTS)

On 9 September 1958 Standard 4MT 4-6-0 No. 75042 stands outside Bedford loco shed. Eighty of these engines were built between 1951 and 1957. Six have survived into preservation. No. 75042 is not among them. It is difficult to see why this class was built at all since there was both a Standard 5MT 4-6-0 and a Standard 4MT 2-6-0 and the latter had the same route availability as the 4MT 4-6-0. (Photo Peter Groom)

Between 1875 and 1908 the MR built no less than 935 0-6-0 goods engines all of the same basic type. Various re-buildings took place over the years, giving some larger boilers and thus a higher power rating, like the two examples pictured here at Bedford loco shed in 1961. No. 43474 had been withdrawn the day before this photograph was taken, on 19 March, while No. 43435, which was actually the older machine, survived for another year. (Photo courtesy RCTS)

In April 1959 Railbus No. M79972 stands at Bedford Midland Road with the 14.36 Bedford to Hitchin. Three of these Park Royal railbuses were allocated to Bedford, when new in 1958, to work the lines to Hitchin and Northampton. They were equipped with a 11.3 litre six-cylinder BUT engines and could seat fifty. They were not reliable and were often replaced by a steam-hauled train. All were withdrawn by 1967. The Bedford–Hitchin line closed to passengers in 1961 and to freight in 1964. (Photo courtesy RCTS)

Although by Bedford trains had got over the Chilterns, their climbing was not finished. Shortly after Bedford they had to surmount Sharnbrook Summit which involved a climb of nearly 5 miles mostly at 1 in 119. The gradient was less pronounced on the slow lines, which passed through Wymington Tunnel. One of the slow lines has now been removed. The mainstay of express services on the MML was the Jubilees. This is Stanier Jubilee 6P 4-6-0 No. 45612 *Jamaica* at Sharnbrook with steam to spare. Note the Fowler tender. The train is the 14.00 St Pancras to Leeds. (Photo Ben Brooksbank)

The Nickey Line

In 1877, after a number of false starts, the MR constructed a line from just north of Harpenden station to Hemel Hempstead. There were just two stations – Redbourn and Hemel Hempsted (note spelling). The connection to the main line only gave access northbound. The reason for this being the importance of freight traffic bound for Luton. Trains from the branch stopped at Chiltern Green to give passengers access to London-bound trains. As the Luton bound freight traffic declined, the connection was reversed in 1888 to give trains access to Harpenden station, where a bay platform was added. This is an early twentieth century view of Redbourn station.

Hemel Hempsted station, a view also dating from the early twentieth century. In 1880 the MR extended the line beyond Hemel Hempsted to the Duckhall Gas Works. There was never a proper connection to the LNWR at Boxmoor, as Hemel Hempstead LNW station was then known. Freight could only be transferred by use of a turntable. This arrangement only lasted until 1897 when the turntable was removed.

In 1906 the MR opened new halts at Heath Park (the effective terminal station of the line), Beaumont's Halt and Godwin's Halt. Roundwood Halt followed in 1927. Passenger services had ceased in 1947 but the line remained open for freight. On 10 August 1958 the RCTS included the branch in their 'Northern and Eastern' railtour. The train is seen at Heath Park Halt behind 3F 0-6-0 No. 43245. Health and Safety was not much of an issue in those days! (Photo Ben Brooksbank)

The line was progressively cut back, leaving, by 1968, only the section from Cupid Green to Harpenden. This was to serve the Hemelite Concrete Company which leased the line from British Railways. This arrangement lasted until 1979, at which time BR demanded a large sum to renew the connection to the main line, which the company was unwilling to pay. The junction was severed on 1 July 1979. Before that, on 19 June 1976, there was another RCTS tour, this time behind Vulcan Foundry 0-6-0 No. D145. The train is at Redbourn station. The line is now a path and cycle way. (Photo courtesy RCTS)

The Great Western/
Great Central Joint Line

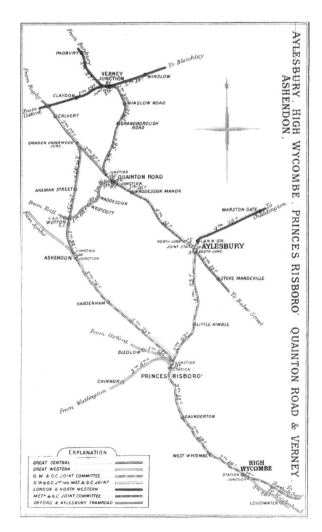

Clearing House map of the lines
around Princes Risborough and
Aylesbury.

The GW/GC Joint line started out life as the Wycombe Railway. Authorised by an Act of 1846 its line ran from a junction with the GWR London–Reading main line near the present location of Taplow station. There were stations at Maidenhead Boyne Hill, Furze Platt, Cookham, Bourne End, Wooburn Green, Loudwater and High Wycombe. Built to the broad gauge, the line was completed by 1854. It was worked from the outset by the GWR. The photograph shows the line at High Wycombe before the new works of the GW/GC line had started. The line was converted to standard gauge in 1870 but the broad-gauge sleepering method was retained.

Loudwater Station.

W.H.A. 3837

On 4 May 1969 BR closed the section of line between Bourne End and High Wycombe. This entailed the closure of Wooburn Green and Loudwater, seen here. Notice the ringed signal on the Up Loop. These signals were used where a siding or loop led on to a running line. Little more than a Hamlet when the railway opened, today Loudwater is effectively a suburb of High Wycombe.

Frustrated at difficulties encountered sharing the GC/Met Joint line, the GCR came to an agreement with the GWR to build a new joint line. The sections of joint line would be Northolt Junction to Ashendon Junction and Princes Risborough to Aylesbury. The GWR would build its own lines from Northolt Junction to Old Oak Common and from Ashendon Junction to Aynho. The GCR would build a line from Neasden South Junction to Northolt Junction and another from Ashendon Junction to Grendon Underwood Junction, where it would gain access to the previously built London Extension. This is West Ruislip, one of the new stations on the joint line. Like a number of the stations on the new lines, West Ruislip was constructed with two through lines, which it still retained in 1989. One of the through lines was subsequently removed.

Denham station under construction. Work started in 1901 and the station opened in 1906 with the completion of the line. The branch to Uxbridge opened in 1907. The station at High Street, competing with two other Uxbridge stations, was never very successful and closed to passengers in 1939. Freight lingered on into the 1960s. The junction with the branch was not actually at the station but one mile to the east.

Denham Golf Club was opened in 1912 at the request of the local club. On 30 May 1989 a Class 115 unit arrives with an Aylesbury–Marylebone service. Notice the 'Pagoda' cast-iron platform shelters. Once common on the GWR these are the last surviving pair on the national network. They are listed structures. A number of other stations opened and/or closed over the years. West Wycombe was one of the original Wycombe Railway stations. It closed in 1958. Dorton Halt opened in 1937, Ilmer Halt in 1929, and South Aylesbury Halt in 1933. All closed in 1963.

At Gerrard's Cross in 1989 the centre through roads are in the process of being removed. By this time with much reduced traffic – the loss of through trains to the Midlands and the disappearance of freight – and the need to re-signal, the through lines were felt to be unnecessary. Since that time there has been a resurgence of passenger traffic, with eight trains an hour passing in each direction, as well as freight and special trains.

Seer Green opened as Beaconsfield Golf Links Halt on 1 January 1915. It became Seer Green in 1918, Seer Green and Jordans in 1950, before reverting to Seer Green in 1974. At Seer Green on 25 March 1950 is the interesting sight of a GC-designed engine running on a GC line that isn't a GC engine at all but rather an ex-GW locomotive! This Robinson-designed 2-8-0 No. 3043 was one of a number built for the Railway Operating Department during the First World War. It was acquired by the GWR in 1925. (Photo Ben Brooksbank)

High Wycombe in 1989. A service for Marylebone stands at the Up platform. On the extreme right is the line for the bay platform and in the foreground the Down platform line. The centre through roads were still extant at this time.

The signals seen in the distance in the previous photograph. On the left are the Up starting signals. The signal for the crossover from Up platform to Up main has been pulled off for the train which has just departed. On the right are the Inner Home signals.

Since 1977 household waste from London and as far afield as Bristol has been dumped into a landfill facility at the former brickworks at Calvert. At one time up to five trains a day would arrive conveying yellow containers each holding 14 tons of household waste. One of the last regular turns for Class 45s in the south were the Northolt–Calvert household waste 'Binliners', that conveniently ran during the middle of the day on Saturdays in the 1980s. On the 3 January 1987, Class 45 No. 45070 catches the setting sun as it heads through High Wycombe with the return empty working from Calvert. (Photo Peter Lovell)

It is 2015 and the through lines have long gone. At the beginning of that year Chiltern Railways (a subsidiary of DB) surprisingly opted to lease new Class 68s from DRS to replace the Class 67s leased from DB Schenker. Six of the class (Nos 68010–68015) are painted in Chiltern Railways Mainline grey livery and equipped to operate with Mk III stock and DVTS. Two other Class 68s (Nos 68008/68009) have also been equipped but have retained their DRS blue livery. On the 12 May 2015, Class 68 No. 68015 propels the 15.55 Birmingham Moor St–Marylebone away from High Wycombe. (Photo Peter Lovell)

While Chiltern Railways refurbished Mk III stock for the Marylebone–Birmingham–Kidderminster services with automatic plug doors, a set of original 'slam door' blue and grey Mk IIIs was retained for a rush hour Marylebone–Banbury service. DRS liveried Class 68 No. 68008 is seen descending to High Wycombe, having just emerged from Whitehouse Tunnel with the 17.50 Marylebone–Banbury on 30 July 2015. (Photo Peter Lovell)

Saunderton was not one of the original stations of the Wycombe Railway. It opened on 1 July 1901. In this early view the Up signal has been pulled off and a train is approaching the station.

A similar view from 2019. In March 2013 the suffragettes burnt down the Down platform buildings, which is presumably why they are no longer there. The footbridge has survived, though without its roof, and so has the waiting room on the Up platform. This building is looked after by the local passengers and contains a fascinating collection of photographs and articles about the station and the line.

Between Saunderton and Princes Risborough is the summit of the GW/GC Joint Line where the tracks diverge. The southbound line follows a lower profile through a short tunnel and gradients of no more than 1 in 164, while the northbound line descends at 1 in 88 approaching Princes Risborough. On 27 August 2013 Class 59 No. 59205 in DB Schenker red livery heads south with the 10.16 Calvert–Neasden empty household waste containers. (Photo Peter Lovell)

Since the rationalisation of the GW/GC Joint Line in the 1990s traffic levels have increased considerably and there is little spare capacity for charter and additional services. Paths for steam railtour operators to run trains calling at Chiltern line stations have proved impossible. On the 16 May 2015, preserved Deltic No. D9009 *Alycidon* made a rare appearance with the Belmond British Pullman set on a 07.56 London Victoria–Kidderminster charter to visit the Severn Valley Railway. (Photo Peter Lovell)

After the opening of the new GWR line from Ashendon Junction to Aynho in 1910, Princes Risborough became a busy junction. This new line gave a route between London and Birmingham 18½ miles shorter than the old route via Oxford and a saving of twenty minutes in journey time. As well as the through route there were branches to Oxford, to Watlington and to Aylesbury. In this 1989 view looking north, a service is just arriving from Aylesbury. The line to Aylesbury can be seen on the right and the branch to Thame curves round the back of the signal box.

Another photograph taken on the same day shows the single platform in use for both Up and Down trains. On the left is the disused Down platform. The signal box is still active, though reduced to seventy levers.

The same view exactly thirty years later. Much has changed. The Down platform has been brought back into use, connected by a new footbridge. Colour light signalling controlled from Marylebone has replaced the semaphores. The track layout has been much simplified. The signal box has survived and been restored by a group of volunteers. It will eventually control Chinnor & Princes Risborough Railway trains which currently use the other face of the Down platform. It is also intended that signal box will act as a museum and be open to visitors.

On 22 September 1956 ex-GW railcar No. W13W stands at the Up platform at Princes Risborough. It is almost certainly engaged on branch line duty. Between 1934 and 1942 the GWR built thirty-eight of these single railcars, in various configurations. No. W13W dates from 1936. It was powered by a pair of 130 hp AEC engines and could seat seventy. It was withdrawn in 1960. (Photo courtesy RCTS)

The same year that W13W was withdrawn saw the introduction of its successor the Class 121 (55000) Bubblecar. They were last used for commercial passenger operations on the national network by Chiltern Railways for the rush hour services between Princes Risborough and Aylesbury, releasing a Class 165. No. 121034 was owned by the Birmingham Transport Museum and, repainted in its original 1960s BR livery, is seen waiting to depart from Princes Risborough for Aylesbury on the evening of 15 January 2016. Note that the destination blind displays 'Llandudno'! (Photo Peter Lovell)

Fast forward forty years to the introduction of the Class 168/3 units, part of the Class 168 Clubman family. The Class 168/3 units are actually Class 170 units that have been adapted to integrate with the rest of the Chiltern fleet. Each vehicle is powered by a 422 hp MTU diesel engine, giving the unit a top speed of 100 mph. On 30 June 2019, unit No. 168326 heads a service from Birmingham Moor Street through Princes Risborough.

The introduction of locomotive-hauled services by Chiltern Railways on Marylebone–Birmingham–Kidderminster was welcomed by enthusiasts and the travelling public alike. Locomotives are normally on the north end of the consist, making photography tricky at times. For a while in 2012 engineering work and diversions saw the sets turned, placing the locomotive at the south end. On 22 May Class 67 No. 67018, in red DB Schenker livery, approaches Princes Risborough as it propels the 08.37 Marylebone–Birmingham Moor Street. (Photo Peter Lovell)

Wotton seen from a passing train in 1950. The station opened in 1906 following the construction of the GC new line from Ashendon Junction to Grendon Underwood, thus giving the tiny hamlet of Wotton Underwood its second station, the first being on the Brill Tramway. It closed on 7 December 1953. (Photo Lamberhurst)

Akeman Street was identical in construction to Wotton and also opened in 1906. Again, we see the two through lines and a shelter on each platform. The station was on an embankment and the main station building was at road level. The photograph shows the station while still under construction. It closed as early as 1930. The Ashendon Junction to Grendon Underwood line closed in 1967.

Princes Risborough to Oxford

Thame station with its overall roof, seen in 1959. Although there is double track through the station, the line, in fact, never had more than a single track with passing loops. The extension of the Wycombe Railway from Princes Risborough to Oxford was authorised by an Act of 1861. Thame was reached in 1862 and Kennington Junction on the Didcot–Oxford line in 1864. There were intermediate stations at Bledlow, Thame, Tiddington (from 1866), Wheatley, and Littlemore. (Photo Lamberhurst)

Thame in the severe winter of 1962/63. A GWR Prairie tank stands ready to depart. This was the last winter of passenger operations with services ending on 7 January. (Photo Lamberhurst)

Tiddington was the next station west of Thame. There was no crossing loop here but there were sidings for freight. A signal box was provided in 1892 but this was downgraded to a ground frame in 1907. Tiddington, along with the other stations on the line, closed to passenger traffic in 1963 but remained open for freight until 1968, when the line between Thame and Morris Cowley was closed to all traffic.

The Wycombe Railway was built to the broad gauge but was rebuilt to standard gauge in 1870. The conversion was achieved in just one week. By this time the WR had been absorbed by the GWR. This is Wheatley station in 1959. (Photo Lamberhurst)

In 1908 the GWR opened a number of halts. These were at Horspath, Garsington Bridge and Iffley. They were closed in 1915 as a wartime measure. In 1928 Morris Cowley station was opened on the site of Garsington Bridge Halt. In 1933 Horspath reopened to be joined by Towersey Halt. Iffley did not reopen. A couple struggle to get off the platform at Horspath Halt in the winter of 1962/63. (Photo Lamberhurst)

The line from Princes Risborough remained open as far as Thame to serve the oil depot there. In 1980 Brush Class 31 Nos 31138 and 31185 thread their way through the pointwork at Princes Risborough with a train of tanks from the Thame depot. The branch closed in 1991.

The Watlington Branch

The Watlington & Princes Risborough Railway received its Act on 26 July 1869. The creation of the company was partly a response to the failure of the Wallingford & Watlington Railway to get any further than Wallingford. The railway opened on 15 August 1872 with a service of three returns daily. At Watlington a Class 2021 saddle tank is arriving at the station. These saddle tanks were converted to pannier tanks in the early years of the twentieth century.

Aston Rowant station in 1959. The other intermediate station was Chinnor. The railway was permanently in financial trouble and the GWR, which in any case hired the locomotives and rolling stock to the company, took over the W&PRR in 1883. (Photo Lamberhurst)

In 1906 the GWR opened three new halts. These were at Bledlow Bridge (seen here) Kingston Crossing and Lewknor Bridge. A further halt at Wainhill Crossing was added in 1925. (Photo Lamberhurst)

Closure to passengers came on 1 July 1957 but the line remained open to freight. In 1959, at Kingston Crossing, a pannier tank is seen with an unidentified freight train. In 1960 the line beyond Chinnor was closed to all traffic, while the section between Princes and Risborough was retained to service the Rugby Portland Cement Works at Chinnor. This traffic ceased in 1989. (Photo Lamberhurst)

In 1990 the Chinnor & Princes Risborough Railway took over the 3½-mile line as a heritage project. It ran its first train in 1994. It has ambitions to extend to Aston Rowant. On 30 June 2019 ex-GWR Small Prairie 2-6-2T No. 5526 is seen near Bledlow with a Princes Risborough–Chinnor service. This locomotive was withdrawn from BR service in 1962, after which it spent twenty-three years in Woodham's scrapyard before being bought and restored to working order.

The Metropolitan/Great Central Joint Line

Pulling away from Marylebone, on 4 June 1963, with a service for Nottingham is 15E Leicester's Stanier Black Five 4-6-0 No. 44848. No less than eighteen Black Fives have been preserved. No. 44848 was not among them and was withdrawn from Rose Grove in February 1968 and scrapped later the same year. (Photo Peter Groom)

At Neasden South Junction, Thomson B1 4-6-0 No. 61369 heads towards London with the 8.30 Manchester London Road to Marylebone on 2 May 1959. In the background on the right is the London Underground Depot. The lines to the left are the GW/GC Joint lines via Princes Risborough. (Photo Ben Brooksbank)

The same scene thirty years later, on 30 May 1989, as a Class 115 DMU, partially repainted in Network South East colours, passes with an Aylesbury–Marylebone service. The signal box is still there and so is the LUL depot, though now obscured by tree growth. A road bridge carrying Great Central Way has been built across the GW/GC lines. The signal box was later abolished.

The Great Central used the Metropolitan lines from Quainton Road to Harrow on the Hill, but from the latter location it had its own independent lines into Marylebone. Neasden South is on this section. It was also the junction for the connecting line to the Great Western at Northolt Junction, opened by the GCR in 1906. On 30 May 1989 Brush-type 4, later Class 47, No. 47468 has reversed from the Acton Wells line on to the main line and now sets off to London with its short rake of tanks. Notice the rather nice GCR bracket signal.

From Harrow on the Hill to Amersham the LNER, then BR, used the electrified lines of the Metropolitan Railway. Harrow to Rickmansworth was electrified in 1925, with Amersham and Chesham following in 1960. Shortly before the end of main line services, on 20 August 1966, Stanier 5MT 4-6-0 No. 44858 is seen near Moor Park with a train heading for Marylebone. (Photo Peter Groom)

Following the extension of electrification to Rickmansworth in 1925 it became the new location for the changeover from electric to steam haulage. Previously this had occurred at Harrow on the Hill. In 1934 Metropolitan H Class 4-4-4T No. 107 stands in the station with a rake of 'Dreadnought' coaching stock. These eight engines were designed by the Metropolitan's Chief Mechanical Engineer Charles Jones and built in 1920/21 by Kerr Stuart & Company. Originally numbered 103 to 110, they were renumbered 6415 to 6422 following the takeover by the LNER of services north of Amersham. They were later moved to other parts of the LNER system before being scrapped in the 1940s.

On 2 September 1961 Metropolitan-Vickers electric locomotive No. 18 *Michael Faraday* heads towards Rickmansworth. It is hauling a rake of 'Dreadnought' carriages. Notice the pick-up shoe on the first carriage. This was connected to the locomotive and was fitted to help prevent 'gapping'. The locomotive, one of a class of twenty, was built in 1922/23. These 1,200 hp locomotives had a top speed of 65 mph. All were withdrawn by 1962, after the introduction of 'A' stock multiple units. (Photo courtesy RCTS)

Standing at platform 3 at Chalfont and Latimer station in July 1948 is push-pull fitted, Robinson C13 4-4-2T No. 7418 with the Chesham Branch service. These Ashbury carriages date from 1898. Between 1906 and 1924 they were converted into electric multiple units. The electrical equipment was later removed when they returned to being hauled vehicles. Two sets of these carriages were used on the Chesham Branch. Following electrification of the branch in 1960 one of the sets was sold to the Bluebell Railway where it remains to this day. No. 7418 survived until 1958, after fifty-five years of service.

Eleven years later the Ashbury coaches are still in use, this time in the charge of Ivatt 2MT 2-6-2T No. 41272, which is propelling the train out of the Chesham Branch platform at Chalfont and Latimer. Between 1946 and 1952 130 of this class were built, first by the LMS and then by BR. In 1959 No. 41272 was a 14D Neasden engine. It later went to the Southern Region before ending its days at Skipton, from where it was withdrawn in 1965. (Photo Ben Brooksbank)

Passengers no longer need to change at Chalfont and Latimer as Chesham Branch services run direct from either Aldgate or Baker Street. There is a half-hourly service during most of the day. On 4 June 2019 an 'S' stock train sits at the pleasant little station of Chesham. These trains, built by Bombardier, were introduced in 2010. The 3.89-mile Chesham Branch opened in 1889. Today the station has just a single platform, but it originally had a bay, which has now been turned into a garden and can be seen on the left.

One year before electrification reached Amersham, on 19 May 1959 Stanier 5MT 4-6-0 No. 45215 stops at the station with the 13.30 stopping service from Marylebone. The Metropolitan Railway started as a line from Paddington to King's Cross and the City. In 1868 a branch was opened to Swiss Cottage by the Metropolitan and St John's Wood Railway. Further extensions followed: to Harrow on the Hill in 1880, to Rickmansworth in 1887, to Amersham in 1889, and to Aylesbury in 1892, where the Metropolitan met the Aylesbury & Buckingham Railway. (Photo Ben Brooksbank)

A Class 115 DMU forming a Marylebone to Aylesbury service approaches the Metropolitan Railway signal box at Great Missenden. The box was abolished in 1994 and control of the area came under Marylebone IECC. In 2010 the box was moved to the Mid Hants Railway.

Some years earlier, in the 1950s, platform lengthening and other works are being carried out. Note the similarity between the water tower here and the one at Chesham. A steam-hauled freight train waits in the Down loop. The loop no longer exists.

Wendover station at the turn of the twentieth century. A Down train stands at the platform. Wendover is deep in the Chiltern Hills and southbound trains have a climb from Aylesbury of nearly 7 miles at up to 1 in 117 before reaching the summit. The line then falls for 4 miles before rising to a second summit at Amersham. In 1895 Wendover 'enjoyed' a basic two hourly service from Baker Street. Very few trains went beyond Aylesbury and in most cases a change of trains was required to reach Quainton Road or Verney Junction.

More than 100 years later and, apart from the motive power, almost nothing has changed. The buildings, the canopies, the cast-iron footbridge all remain the same. At the platform a Class 165/0 unit stands with the 12.57 from Marylebone to Aylesbury Parkway on 3 July 2019. These 'Turbo' units were introduced in 1990 to replace the Class 115 DMUs on the Chilterns lines. Each vehicle is equipped with a 350 hp Perkins 2006-TWH diesel engine, giving a total of 1,050 hp for a three-car unit. Today the line enjoys a half hourly service between Marylebone and Aylesbury/Parkway throughout the day.

The first station at Aylesbury was Aylesbury High Street, the terminus of the London and Birmingham branch from Cheddington. This station opened in 1838. Next to arrive, in 1863, was the GWR branch from High Wycombe which had its own station at Aylesbury Town. The Aylesbury & Buckingham Railway shared this station from 1868. When the Metropolitan arrived in 1892 it built its own station at Brook Street but two years later its trains were diverted into Aylesbury Town and Brook Street was closed. The station seen in this photograph dates from 1926, when Aylesbury Town was comprehensively rebuilt.

This photograph of ex-GCR B3 4-6-0 No. 6164 *Earl Beatty* was taken between 1927 and 1939, while No. 6164 and two other members of the class were allocated to Neasden. In 1939 No. 6164 was rebuilt with Caprotti valve gear. This was an attempt to reduce coal consumption in what was one of Robinson's less successful locomotives. No. 6164 is waiting to leave Aylesbury with what was probably an overnight express from Manchester. To allow its London Extension access to the capital, the GCR entered into an agreement to use the tracks of the Metropolitan Railway. The GCR had its own tracks from Harrow on the Hill to Marylebone. Initially the GCR only had running powers but in 1906 the lines became Joint property.

At Aylesbury, on 22 July 1961, ex-LNER K3 2-6-0 No. 61913 stands with the 16.46 departure to Marylebone. No. 61913 was a 2F Woodford Halse engine at this time and would be withdrawn from that shed, just seven months later. The K3s were introduced by Gresley as fast goods engines for the GNR in 1920. They continued to be built by the LNER and altogether a total of 193 were constructed between 1920 and 1937. They had a strangely out-of-proportion appearance due to the 6-ft boilers seeming too large in comparison with the 5-ft 8-in. drivers. (Photo courtesy RCTS)

A view looking south from Aylesbury station on 30 May 1989 as a Class 115 DMU arrives with a service from Marylebone via Amersham. The line on the right is from Princes Risborough. Work is already under way on re-signalling the line, as part of which the tracks here will be remodelled and the signal box abolished.

The long rod attached to the boiler of ex-GC F1 2-4-2T No. 5594 was part of the less than successful mechanical push-pull apparatus fitted in 1922. No. 5594 is seen in LNER days standing at Aylesbury with the motor train for Verney Junction. Of considerable interest is the twelve-wheel coach behind the locomotive, which looks to be of foreign manufacture.

Quainton Road station came into being with the opening of the Aylesbury & Buckingham Railway on 23 September 1868, which was worked from the outset by the GWR. In 1891 the A&B was taken over by the Metropolitan Railway, which reached Aylesbury in 1892. Through running between Baker Street and Verney Junction began in 1897. This view looking south dates from the 1930s. Just visible standing at the Brill platform, at the head of a mixed train, is the 4-4-0T Metropolitan A-Class locomotive No. 41 (works No. 865), one of six A-Class engines built by Beyer Peacock in 1869. Note the long line of coal wagons in the background. The grassed enclosure behind the down platform is a livestock pen.

Quainton Road was closed to passengers on 4 March 1963. Trains on the GCR main line continued to pass through, as here with Stanier 5MT 4-6-0 No. 44920 with the 14.38 Marylebone to Nottingham service on 22 June 1966. Main line operations ceased later the same year. (Photo courtesy RCTS)

Quainton Road station today. In 1962 the London Railway Preservation Society was set up with a base at Quainton Road, later absorbed into the Quainton Railway Society which now operates the Buckinghamshire Railway Centre. The station has remained largely unchanged since closure and all the buildings, including the shelter on the Brill branch platform, are listed. Things will change in the future as it is intended that passenger trains will once again run north of Aylesbury as part of the East West Rail Project and a number of changes will have to be made for safety reasons.

Winslow Road was on the A&BR line from Aylesbury to Verney Junction – the A&BR never did reach Buckingham. From 1906 services were provided jointly by the GCR and the Met. In 1933 the Met became part of the London Passenger Transport Board, which withdrew passenger services beyond Quainton Road in 1936. The line to Verney Junction closed completely in 1947. On the last day of passenger service ex-GE F7 2-4-2T No. 8307 stands at the station with the auto-train, waiting to depart to Verney Junction. Notice once again the mysterious twelve-wheeled carriage.

Heading a long train of coal trucks near Verney Junction is Metropolitan K Class 2-6-4T No. 115. Six locomotives of this class were built by Armstrong Whitworth in 1925 using parts made at Woolwich Arsenal to SECR designs. In fact, they were almost identical to the SECR K (River) Class. In 1937 the engines were sold to the LNER, becoming Class L2. None survived beyond 1948.

The Brill Branch

A very early photograph of an Aveling & Porter 0-4-0, on the Brill branch, hauling an assortment of vehicles, including a four-wheel brake and two cattle wagons. The Wotton Tramway was built to serve the estate of the Duke of Buckingham. The 4-mile-long line to Wotton was in use by 1871, trains originally being horse-drawn. By 1872 the line had been extended a further 2½ miles to Brill and a passenger service started.

Waddesdon station became Waddesdon Road from 1922. At the same time Waddesdon Manor on the Metropolitan/Great Central Joint line became Waddesdon. In 1883 the Duke of Buckingham proposed extending the tramway to Oxford and the Act authorising the extension was passed in August that year. The Oxford, Aylesbury & Metropolitan Junction Railway Company was set up, but the investment didn't come forward. Under the scheme Waddesdon Road station would have disappeared.

In 1894 the tramway was taken over by the Oxford & Aylesbury Tramroad. It was that company which introduced two Manning Wardle K Class 0-6-0 saddle tanks to the line. Seen here at the branch platform at Quainton Road is Brill No. 1 (Manning Wardle No. 1249). At that time the fare from Quainton Road to Brill was sixpence halfpenny and the journey took about forty minutes.

This is Westcott in the 1930s. The train has arrived hauled by one of the Metropolitan Class A tanks. At this time there was a service of four trains on weekdays with an additional service on Saturdays. Journey time was about thirty-two minutes. Trains stopped as required at both Westcott and Wood Siding.

In 1899 the line came under Metropolitan Railway control and in 1903 the Manning Wardle tanks were replaced by two Metropolitan Railway D Class engines. These in turn were replaced by two 'A' Class engines, Nos 23 and 41. These 4-4-0Ts were built by Beyer-Peacock for use on the Metropolitan sub-surface lines. Made redundant by electrification, they had their condensing equipment removed and a cab added. No. 41 is seen at Wood Siding. No. 23 survived into preservation and is to be found at the London Transport Museum.

In 1933 the Metropolitan Railway became part of the London Passenger Transport Board and it was decided to terminate all passenger services beyond Aylesbury from 1935. So it was that the Brill branch finally succumbed. The photograph shows the Brill terminus in the last year of service. One of the Class A tanks is at the head of the train.